NO REGRETS

Living the Single and Saved Life

DARYL B. ANDERSON

NO REGRETS

Living the Single and Saved Life

DARYL B. ANDERSON

Lithonia, GA

© 2018 Daryl B. Anderson

All rights reserved.

No part of this publication may be reproduced, stored in a retrieval system or transmitted in any form or by any means, electronic, mechanical, photocopying, recording or otherwise, without the expressed written permission of the publisher.

Scripture references are taken from various versions and translations of the Holy Bible. Pronouns for referring to the Father, Son and Holy Spirit are capitalized intentionally and the words satan and devil are never capitalized.

Publisher:
MEWE, LLC
www.mewellc.com

First Edition
ISBN: 9781732432727

Library of Congress Control Number: 2018960016

Printed in the United States of America.

*To my Lord and Savior Jesus Christ,
all glory and praises to you.*

In memory of my Grandmother Elizabeth, known to my family as "My Mama," and my mother Janet Anderson; you both are always with me!

To my daughters Tiffany, Ashleigh, and Rashanda, my sister Andre, my brother Johnnie, my grandson Ryleigh Daryl, family and friends; thank you for your support.

CONTENTS

Acknowledgements ix

Foreword xi

Introduction xiii

Chapter 1 - Living Single and Saved 1

Chapter 2 - The Changing Views of the Church 11

Chapter 3 - Divorce: A Blessing or a Sin 21

Chapter 4 - Looking for Love in All the Wrong Places 33

Chapter 5 - The Pitfalls of Single Life 45

Postlude 55

About the Author 59

ACKNOWLEDGEMENTS

I am grateful for the men who helped mentor me over the years: Uncle Raymond Anderson, the Late Deacon Unis W. Vinson, the Late Archbishop Jimmie Lee Smith, and the Late Bishop Eddie L. Long.

Special thanks to the Late Marvin "Doc" Frady for his spirited wisdom.

I am also very grateful for the Word of Life and Smyrna Worship Center church families.

FOREWORD

No Regrets, by Bishop Daryl Anderson captures and articulates quite eloquently some of the fundamental social and ecclesiastical mazes that "singles" in the twenty first century Christian community must navigate. The preponderance of Scriptural illuminations concerning misconceptions of singleness as well as the choice of personal chastity is not only refreshing, but also beneficial to whoever will spend the time to read this book.

The writer addresses the matter of "LIVING SINGLE AND SAVED" from the informed position of both a married and a single pastor. This unique perspective gives him an authentic voice, providing insight into the plight and challenges Christian singles face as well as the pain they endure.

I highly recommend *No **Regrets*** to single Christians who are trying to make sense of their singleness, as well as couples and Christian counselors as a valuable addition to their resource libraries.

The heartiest congratulations to Bishop Daryl Anderson, again on a book well written!

Desmond Whittaker
Light of the World
Grand Cayman Islands

INTRODUCTION

Some Christians, who are experiencing problems in their marriages, find little help because one or both partners are involved in ministry. Many times, those who assist such persons are themselves dealing with hidden troubles and crises.

Having to pastor a congregation, while at the same time maintaining your family life is a struggle. Moreover, addressing your family's private problems in public can be challenging.

Can a pastor be divorced, yet, counsel those who are married? How would other pastors view him/her? How would the congregation and others feel about the situation?

Though there are varying perspectives on marriage and divorce in the church, the reality is that many churchgoers shun those who are divorced believing they may have failed God and should have remained in their marriages no matter what its issues.

I can attest to this because I was divorced and have yet to remarry. Some took my new status to mean that I had returned to a sinful life. The general perception was that I could not be both single and repentant.

Typically, the transition from being married to single is tasking for both parties. However, going through a divorce with the church's involvement is extra difficult. Members tend to take sides – some for the spouse; others for the pastor. These are often the same people both persons offered spiritual guidance to in some way.

What further complicates matters for pastors is that they often make it seem as though their married lives are unproblematic. On the surface, it appears as if they have the perfect, fairytale relationship. But underneath it all, pastors have the same issues as everyone else. However, they simply seldom express them to the church.

On the other hand, singles in the church are often thought to be lonely and unhappy. In fact, some believe that certain tasks in the church cannot be performed by an unmarried or single individual. They believe such positions are reserved for married people. It's like a woman, who after a certain age is childless or unmarried; people assume that something must be wrong with her. What they fail to come to grips with is that some singles are, in fact, quite content with their lives. Their singlehood doesn't mean they do not or will never want a relationship, either. Singles come to church with the same objectives as married people: to seek a better spiritual life through God and to work with others to achieve it. They decidedly do not attend church to be judged on their relationship status!

In some instances, married women and men can be so insecure; they are apprehensive about allowing singles to converse with or even be in the presence of their spouses. Furthermore, they do not invite them to their homes. These kinds of mindsets create challenges for single men and women in the church. Hence, the most difficult part about being saved and single is not being saved. It is not even attempting to live a holy and disciplined life. Rather, it is trying to stay grounded around other Christians who are in relationships and who judge you because you are not.

Where the Spirit of God resides, there is freedom. My grandmother always used to say, "God doesn't change, but people do." How much have you grown in God compared to your spouse? How much has the congregation grown spiritually as compared to the pastor? How much have the people in the fellowship grown in relation to one another?

Not all pastors are counselors or authorities on marriage. Therefore, it is entirely possible they will receive or give inaccurate or incorrect spiritual advice based on their personal interpretations of the Bible.

I think the burdens we impose on ourselves by sparing thoughts for how others perceive us, as well as by seeking to uphold the standards of our ministries, bring additional problems to our personal lives. One such example is the prevailing thought among Christians that the spouse of a pastor must look and act the part of the pastor's church's "First Lady."

As pastors, we sometimes force our spouses to assume this position because we consider it fitting for the church. Unfortunately, this has inadvertently compromised the integrity of countless marriages, even if the couple stays together. Outward appearances, then, have seemingly become more important than our happiness. God never instructed us to stay in unfulfilling marriages or lead double lives for the sake of the ministry. What good is offering spiritual counsel to other marriages when our own is neither satisfying nor in a place of peace?

God, through His grace, has and will always save us. Nevertheless, it is possible for life to pitch a fastball that will render us single. Did God not free us from the prison of sin when He died for us on the cross? Should we continue to hold on to guilt or the past because we are single for whatever reason? God's grace, mercy, and forgiveness are for all our sins, not just a few. Being single and saved is not a sin, and even if it were, it is one for which Christ died and from which singles are released.

I have freed myself from how the church perceives me as a bishop. For the first time in my ministry, I no longer feel like I am torn between my family, my former wife, and the church.

I grew up without a father; therefore, I sought guidance in ministry. I also didn't grow up as a saved person. Most of my relationships started from what I experienced and saw in the streets. I was prepared for relationships, yes, but not a Christian relationship, which is harder than any street relationship. The church exerts more pressure on its leaders through its expectations than anyone on the streets ever could.

What happens when God calls you but doesn't call your spouse? In that circumstance, how do you make your spouse a part of the ministry? At times, you may feel like you're not living up to a pastoral life and to the confidence people have in you. There's no manual to read on how best to assume the responsibilities of a pastor or spouse. Most of the training involved is trial and error; you assimilate as much information as you can.

I once thought there were no problems in my home, or at least, it felt that life at home was great. My wife and I were best friends. However, the church may very well have pulled us apart. My spouse's group took her side and my group mine. I often found myself angry with God for His call and not having a father in the ministry or a natural father. I felt slighted by Him. Most of the other pastors had fathers to set the way for them. No one in my family had taken on a pastoral role before. I had no examples of a successful marriage or any marriage to derive inspiration from. Therefore, I tried to adhere to the Bible's teachings as best I could. Despite my attempts, I still had problems – mostly with the church.

If I could do it all over again, I would not want a spouse in the ministry or involved in the church unless I had her consent or support. I would not want her to serve simply because that was God's call for me in my life.

Divorce is a painful, stressful process all on its own. However, when you're in the ministry and going through a divorce those feelings are compounded. You can feel like you've failed God and yourself. Nevertheless, keeping a marriage intact for that reason alone can be equally detrimental. You can feel empty and hypocritical. Indeed, you will be living a double life – untruthful to God, the people around you, those in your ministry, and you.

I hope and pray that as you read each chapter of this book, the Word of God will touch you and bring healing to the broken places in your life. As you read the experiences shared, may you be inspired to move forward in life and ministry.

Each chapter of this book is designed not only to minister to your outward relationships but to help you search yourself. In doing so, you will find the hindrances that stop you from enjoying life as a single and saved person.

This book is thought provoking and filled with many answers to life's questions. You will:

- Understand some misconceptions about being single and saved
- Discover the five things you need to know before getting married
- Find out how to know if you are in a committed relationship
- Learn what is a need-driven relationship
- Learn how to avoid the seven pitfalls of single life

Are you suffering from the emotional scars of past relationships? Do you want to move past the surface and find healing for those deep wounds? This book will help you leave the past behind and move forward in forgiveness with *No Regrets!*

Daryl B. Anderson

CHAPTER 1

LIVING SINGLE AND SAVED

> *But I speak this by permission, and not of commandment For I would that all men were even as I myself. But every man hath his proper gift of God, one after this manner, and another after that. I say therefore to the unmarried and widows, it is good for them if they abide even as I* (See 1 Cor. 7:6-8).

The Apostle Paul tells the Corinthians that it was good, in the juncture of time, for Christians to keep themselves single. Yet he says that marriage and the comforts of the state are settled by divine wisdom. None may break the Law of God, yet the perfect rule leaves men at liberty to serve Him in the way most suited to their power and circumstances of which others are frequently unfit judges. All must determine what is right for themselves, by themselves, seeking counsel from God on how and why they ought to act.

The Apostle Paul asked to speak by permission to the Body of Christ. This serves as a direction to us not to make assumption on the singles in our churches.

Misconceptions about Being Saved and Single

Since my divorce, I have realized that not everyone accepts or feels comfortable with singles in the ministry. This lack of acceptance or discomfort can be attributed to a few misconceptions regarding singlehood and ministry. Some of these are listed below prayerfully to bring a better understanding of what a single may be going through as they live a saved life:

1. **The misconception is that you must be married to be saved and not burn.** *"But if they cannot contain, let them marry: For it is better to marry than to burn"* (I Cor. 7:9 NIV). One can take this "to burn" to mean to burn with passion and not to burn in hell.

2. **The misconception is that your income is more because of less responsibilities.** This is false, especially if the single person has a child or children that they are taking care of. I recall pastoring once that when a vow was given to the church, it did not consider the stress that the single would undergo in trying to come up with the same amount that was accorded to a married couple with at least two streams of income. This places a burden on the single because she/he usually only has one stream of income.

3. **The misconception that all singles, whether female or male, are anxious to be married or in a relationship.** After all, who among us wouldn't love to have someone to share the rest of our lives with, go to dinner or a movie with, or just spend time with; these are wants that are shared by singles and married couples alike. The Apostle Paul writes to the Philippians and to all saints, *"Be careful for nothing; but in everything by prayer and supplication with thanksgiving let your requests be made unto God"* (Ph.1. 4:6).

4. **The misconception that the pastor must have a different sermon for singles and have special events because they need to be addressed in a particular way.** *"Preach the word: be instant in season, out of season: reprove rebuke, exhort with all longsuffering and doctrine"* (1 Tim. 4:2). The Apostle Paul tells Timothy to just preach the word and God's Word will bring the reprove, rebuke and doctrine. It makes no difference, whether you are single or married, when the pastor preaches the Word of God!

5. **The misconception that all marriages must be equally yoked to work.** *"Be ye not unequally yoked together with*

unbelievers: for what fellowship hath righteousness with unrighteousness? And what communion hath light with darkness?" (II Cor. 6:14). In Biblical days, when farmers plowed their fields, they would use an equal yoke. This meant they would use two oxen, or two cows, etc. The yoke was equal, so the animals would pull in a straight line. If you put an ox and mule together it would be crooked. Believers are not to yoke together with unbeliever. The whole concept of being together is that both must pull their share of the load regardless. If both are not working on the same vision, with the same amount of effort, the line will be crooked. Many relationships are failing, not because the two people are not saved, or are unequally yoked in terms of their faith, but because of the lack of love for and commitment to one another.

Some relationships fail because individuals may enter the relationship with different goals that are not properly, or at all, expressed before the relationship begins. This, of course, has deleterious effects on the relationship's integrity. Always remember that being equally yoked also applies to being in the relationship together.

Steve Harvey, a famous talk show host, published a book titled, *Act Like a Lady, Think Like a Man.* There is nothing wrong with this book; I am certain it has worked for many singles in entering committed relationships. Once God brings the two together as one, however, both must have the mind of Christ!

Biblical Teaching

"I would that all men were even as I myself. But everyman hath his proper gift of God, one after this manner, and another after that" (1Corinthians 7:7). The Apostle Paul advises us to marry if we cannot control ourselves. In 1 Corinthians 7 and 8, he gives

strong support for being single when it comes to one's relationship with God. The requirement for being single is that one must have full control over one's feelings of lust, not just sexually but in all areas of life. Self-control is a must.

Being single and saved in today's world and in the Body of Christ does not require a special word from those in authority. Rather, it is the same word that is given to the married couple: that of self-control.

For many years, I pastored as a married man, oblivious of the plight and challenges singles faced, and the pain they endured; some self-inflicted, some by their peers. I pastored from the viewpoint of a married person. What I realize now, is that single people actually go through a considerable amount of pressure in the church when it comes to marriage. It is much like the pressure a woman finds herself under when she does not have children by a certain age.

The Apostle Paul addressed this ever-growing problem as it relates to the Body of Christ. Let me take time to denounce some schemes.

- Every Christian single does not have, nor needs to have, a desire to be married

- Those living the single life are not necessarily gay or on the 'down low'

- Not all singles are lonely; They are not all overly eager in their search for company.

These are just a few of the schemes that a single person may encounter every day. I am by no means speaking for all singles or trying to change the way they are viewed by all people. However, I want to point out that the assumptions that many have about mature singles that are living that life may sometimes be misguided.

Those who have been married or in a committed relationship for an extended period of time may have forgotten what it's like to be single – things may have changed dramatically since the last time they were single. The way people meet, talk, and work is nowhere near what it used to be in the "olden days." If the church and the world have changed, why would we think that dating and living single would not also change? No matter what changes take place in life, God's Word remains the same throughout time.

As a single bishop, I've discovered that it's alright to enjoy life. The first couple of years, I was trying to stay saved and single. This meant not going to movies or dinner with anyone, even if they were just a friend. I began to place unwanted burdens on myself trying to live a life that appeared to be in line with what people may have been thinking.

One day I heard an old song by Cameo from my teenage days that said, "I'm living the single life!" This song said, "I am living!" God said to Moses, "I am that I am." He said "the thief cometh not, but for to steal, and kill, and to destroy; I am come that they may have life (live) more abundantly (See John: 10:10).

While many of us live the single life, it does not mean that God has abandoned us. In fact, as long as we believe in Him, He never will.

Singles Who Are Seeking to Get Married

The Apostle Paul said in 1 Corinthians 7:25-28:

> *Now concerning virgins I have no commandment of the Lord, yet I give my judgement as one that hath obtained mercy of the Lord to be faithful. I suppose therefore that this is good for the present*

distress, I say, that it is good for a man so to be. Art thou bound unto a wife? Seek not a wife. But and if thou marry, thou hast not sinned; and if a virgin marry, she hath not sinned. Nevertheless such shall have trouble on the flesh: but I shall spare you.

The church at Corinth faced a crisis, which Paul had to address in the above letter to the church. These were people who had surrendered themselves to pleasure, debauchery, and drunkenness. In the Roman Empire, if you were "corinthianized," it meant you engaged in sin to a high limit (See 'Thru the Bible' series with Dr. J. Vernon McGee). It was against this corrupt background Paul preached and wrote the books of First and Second Corinthians.

As a young man, I was married in 1982 to a very beautiful young lady. The time and situations were much different from now. We had a lot to overcome starting out, but the job market was not an issue and money was not the main reason for the marriage. Both of us came from well-respected homes where receiving a good education was expected and valued.

What we had as crises don't compare to the crises the younger or older singles face today. Unemployment is high, though some would say otherwise. Couples must deal with lower standards. They have all kinds of health issues and one or both may not have health coverage. Trying to obtain a decent place to live when both members have issues with their credit, or are trying to blend a home together when both may have children outside of the relationship, presents even greater challenges. Many Christians are unequally yoked even when it comes to those of the same faith, depending on how they were raised in church, denominationally speaking.

In this letter to Corinth, Apostle Paul talks about other things, all considering the present distress. He mentioned five things humans experience in this world:

1. **Marriage**

   "Therefore shall a man leave his father and mother, and shall cleave unto his wife; and they shall be one flesh" (Gen. 2:24). It is clear that the Apostle Paul now understands the purpose of marriage in this epistle to the churches, but he was also weary of the present-day circumstances that came between the new couple and factors of family that may come from divorce, children and even in-laws that stay involved with their children. It is unfortunate that some studies indicate divorce is at an all-time high in the Body of Christ.

2. **Sorrow**

   "A time to weep and a time to laugh; a time to mourn and a time to dance" (Ecclesiastes 3:4). Every relationship must endure these times in life. One must understand being married or single doesn't prevent these seasons from coming.

   Being in a relationship where both trust in God and each other helps to make the seasons bearable. It's not what we see on the outside, but what's on the inside of a person that determines how strong they really are. It's in these times of sorrow that bring out the best or worst of an individual.

3. **Joy**

   "Rejoice Evermore. Pray without ceasing. In everything give thanks: for this is the will of God in Christ Jesus concerning you" (Ephesians 5:16-18).

The Apostle Paul gives us the formula for maintaining a healthy relationship with God, ourselves, and one another. After the people heard the reading of the law, they began to weep, but Nehemiah told them *"Neither be ye sorry; for the joy of the Lord is your strength"* (Nehemiah 8:106). Joy in one life is not defined by the material possessions that we have, but by our obedience to the Word of God which carries over into our lives.

4. **Commence**

    The word 'commence' means: begin, start, get down to business, get off the ground. When entering a relationship, we must understand that everyone has a past; many times, we do not address the past and the hurt that might have affected us before entering a relationship. As such, we never really enter a relationship with a fresh state of mind, but instead, we carry our old baggage into it.

5. **Relationship with the World**

    "And be not conformed to this world, but be ye transformed by the renewing of your mind, that ye may prove what is that good, and acceptable, and perfect, will of God" (Roman 12:2). Understanding how to live in this world does not require being in a relationship. As a single, learning how to take care of yourself and family is important. If you depend on the world for your provisions, you will be at a loss as to what to do when things fall apart unexpectedly, or your spouse leaves or passes away. We must learn how to trust God and ourselves. The renewing of the mind commences now, even while you're single. One's mind must change to adapt to married life, and those who are married must

neither think nor act as though they are single, even when their spouse is not around. Being in a committed relationship takes the renewing of one's mind every day.

The Apostle Paul assures singles that it is of course good and proper to marry, but whether you're single or married, everyone must endure these five situations every day!

CHAPTER 2

THE CHANGING VIEWS OF THE CHURCH

Has the church's perception of singles changed materially over the years? For that matter, has the church made any significant progress on how it approaches and interacts with its singles? Who, precisely, does the church consider to be 'single,' in relation to the Word of God? Is everyone without a spouse considered single? How do singles define themselves? Do singles consider themselves single when they are in committed relationships? The church's leadership must directly address ideologies such as these to stay relevant with views of singles in church.

> *But I would have you without carefulness. He that is unmarried doeth for the things that belong to the Lord, how he may please the Lord* (I Cor. 7:32).

The Church and Singles

The Apostle Paul gives us a clear vision of the church's perception of singles; namely, that those who are single and living a believer's life should apply their focus on God. This gives the believer the freedom to serve in any capacity in the church. After all, there are no restrictions on one's freedom to be used by God in his House.

Most of the time, the church misses out on using a single because of preconceived notions of their lifestyle. With married couples, it is presumed that they by default are focused on ministry. This is a misconception that has undoubtedly prevented several singles from taking leadership positions in ministry.

Singles usually don't want to be treated as if they are alone and seeking only a relationship when it comes to serving. One's relationship status should not be a prerequisite for assuming a leadership or other working position in the church.

The Apostle Paul states that a single is more focused and has no hinders to fulfilling their role in serving. It has been my view over the past few years since my divorce that as a single, I have more freedom in serving the Lord. This is not to say that when I was married I experienced difficulties in this area, but I knew my family needed me as the head of the household; every decision I made put them first. Being single, even if only partially, removes that responsibility, thereby giving the single more freedom to serve the Lord.

Being single does not mean that you lack accountability. If anything, there is more accountability because, according to the Bible, we only answer to God. Singles must therefore exercise great discipline because serving the Lord should be their upmost priority!

Most singles want to work in church because it gives them a feeling of responsibility towards their church family. It also is a way of feeling connected to that family, and to something bigger than themselves.

Perhaps it's time for the leadership of the church to reconsider how they utilize singles when it comes to serving in the local church. This may open the conversation between singles and non – singles that may enable both parties to find ways to help meet the needs of the community.

We tend to attract those who experience situations and struggles like our own. If the church truly wants strong representation of singles in its fold, it must bring itself to understand that most singles have friends who are also single, and that some of those friends are neither saved nor attending church frequently (or at all). The church must come to grips with the reality that most of fellowship of singles resides not within the church walls, but outside.

Ultimately, all singles want is a message, not a lecture on what not to do. It is not uncommon for singles to be approached outside the church for various reasons. This trend has caused some singles to build emotional and psychological walls just to insulate themselves from unsolicited advances. This could lead to being or appearing standoffish, not wanting to be open and honest, and not being trusting. For example, a single woman is more likely to receive unsolicited advances daily than a single man.

The church, especially on Sundays, is aware that singles want to come and feel safe. Having said that, I must also say that not all singles who enter the church may want this; some may even approach a married person in an inappropriate way. Just because some singles have not learned how to discipline themselves, however, does not mean that all singles are uncouth in their conduct.

Many singles attend church primarily or only to receive the Word of God and to enter a place to serve God and become actively involved in the church's activities.

In my view, the church should have at least one person in place who singles can converse with while not being made to feel as though they are being accused before the facts are fully ventilated. Otherwise, it is all but a certainty that these singles will abandon the church to not interrupt the House of God; feeling like no one would believe them in that matter. Singles are not a ministry in the church; instead, they make up the church!

Singles in Leadership

"Judge not, that ye not judge. For with what judgement ye judge ye shall be judged and with what measure ye mete, it shall be measured to you again" (Matt. 7:1-2). Being in leadership gives us the ability to discern the nature of one who serves in the church. This may or may not be a good thing; if the ability of a church's leaders to lead and serve is assessed by reference to their marital status, this can prohibit that person from serving to the

fullest. The lasting belief that a single person will invariably have a lifestyle that precludes her/him from either being used by leaders to do God's Work, or becoming leader themselves, has plagued the church for quite some time.

The church, as a body, has, over the years, conjured up a variety of justifications for preventing singles to serve in the church and has made it clear that its stance is that those who are married make better candidates to operate in the church; an opinion based on perceived stability and a decreased likelihood of being spiritually subdued by the desires of their flesh. The Word of God, when identifying the work of the flesh, however, does not distinguish between those who are single and those who are married.

Adultery

The story in John 8:1-11 tells the incident of a woman who was caught in adultery. First, we must define the word 'adultery' to understand the seriousness of the case brought before Jesus.

Old Testament: Adultery was understood to refer to sexual relations between a married (or betrothed) woman and a man other than her husband. It was a sin against the husband.

New Testament: Jesus extended the definition of 'adultery' to include sexual relations between a married man and a woman other than his wife (See I Cor. 6:15-16, I Cor. 7:2).

Therefore, for a believer, adultery is the sin of a married man having sexual relations with anyone other than his wife, or a married woman having sexual relations with anyone other than her husband.

Fornication

The word 'fornication" means to commit illicit sexual intercourse between two people who are not married to one other. In other words, to fornicate is to engage in sexual intercourse while being unmarried. The Bible's teaching on both subjects are throughout scripture (See Gal. 5:19). Those of us who are in leadership positions in the church must be aware that leadership cannot and must not be in judgement of those who God is sending to serve in the church.

Prejudice

Prejudice is a prejudgment or the formation of an opinion on an event or person before being appraised of the relevant facts. The word 'prejudice' is often used to refer to a preconceived or otherwise usually unfavorable judgement towards people or a person because of gender, political opinion, social class, age, disability, religion, sexuality, racial ethnicity, language, nationality, or personal characteristics.

Here is an example of how this can be used to the church's detriment in leadership. Suppose two people serve in the church's leadership. They have the same responsibilities. One is single. The other is married. They both must attend a church meeting on Saturday morning at 9:00 a.m. It's now 9:45 a.m. Neither leader is present at the meeting, at that time. The pastor and members are becoming increasingly frustrated. They are also assuming that the married person has a family, so maybe something happened that's making them late.

The single person, however, does not receive that benefit of the doubt; she/he may have just overslept from Friday night… surely, nothing else could be making her/him run late. These are thoughts commonly held by the leadership, even when they are not buttressed with factual evidence.

Being single in the "olden days" is nothing like it is in the present. An abundance of singles have families of their own, and are raising children by themselves. Many, after going through divorce, loss of a loved one and failed relationships, find themselves not even going out, or find themselves disinterested in the courting or dating scene.

A majority of singles in our society are also parents; parents who must be constantly vigilant about not bringing just anyone around their child or children.

As a single, I just want to be treated fairly by the Body of Christ and viewed as a Child of God, who needs the same message on Sunday as everyone else. I don't want to be singled out as a single person, or to be viewed as lonely and desperate.

I just want to live the single life with no regrets!

Is Commitment a Thing of the Past?

The dictionary definition of 'committed' is *"being dedicated or loyal to something, to give for safe keeping or to be confined."* The word 'confined' means, *"limited or restricted."*

To accept that one is in a committed relationship is to accept that she/he (albeit not by law or God) is limited or restricted to the one person she/he shares that committed relationship with.

> *Therefore, I say to the unmarried and widows, it's good for them if they abide even as I. But if they cannot contain, let them marry; for it is better to marry than to burn* (I Cor. 7:8-9).

The definition for being in a committed relationship has evolved substantially with time. Some persons want to be in a relationship, but not committed to that one person; on the understanding that in God's Eyes, a person is only truly committed to another within the institution of marriage. The reality, however, is that an inconsiderable number of singles are in relationships with those who will not, or do not want to, demonstrate commitment through marriage. When such commitment issues persist in a relationship, one or both of its members can wind up emotionally devastated.

Commitment and trust issues can carry over into the local church. The Word of God must be explained in a way that is accessible and applicable to singles and couples in committed relationships alike. When one person in a committed relationship cheats on the other, it almost always causes problems... not all of which can be resolved entirely. Sometimes, these limitations are not articulated, but are nevertheless implemented and treated with the same sacrosanctity of the limitations of a marriage!

When the church fails to see the emotions tied between two people in a relationship, simply because they are not married, it only adds to the emotional pain they are experiencing. The hope of one day being married is normally within both parties, but what tends to happen is that one party wants to be married more than the other party. (In most cases, the party who longs for marriage more is the female.)

When both parties of a relationship are in Christ, their spirituality may line up with the Word of God, but they will both apply His Word differently. As I stated and will continue to state, the problems which arise for singles, married couples and persons in committed relationships are all the same.

Some churches do not create a distinction between a person who is single and a person who is 'only' in a committed relationship. The married couples attending such churches may view such people as single, lonely, etc.; whereas, in the single's mind, they are of course in a committed relationship that carries the potential to lead to marriage, with the marriage certificate being the only thing needed to 'legitimize' the relationship. It makes sense for a believer to go through this thought process; in the Word of God, marriage is the highest and greatest institution ever created. The church should therefore strive to be able to relate to the perspectives of persons in committed relationships (and I do not intend to downplay the significance of marriage in recommending this).

Commitment is a genuine concept, no matter how or within what context it is practiced. A person in a committed relationship may consider that it is founded on the Word of God and is godly in all but the official respects (e.g. marriage). To some, a commitment in itself is a marriage, or like a marriage; and should you seek to explain the difference, you or the church itself may be rejected in the process.

As a young man growing up in Durham, North Carolina, I remember staying with my grandmother, who was a God-fearing woman. I remember having conversations with her about moving in with my young girlfriend. I pleaded my case to her as to why it would work, as she listened wordlessly. After I was finished, I felt I was convincing in my resolve to move in together with her, but not marry her. My grandmother replied, "If you really loved her, and felt that it was right, you would marry her."

When the time comes, a committed relationship will get you to the place where you feel as though you want to be with that one person for the remainder of your life. For the single and saved, commitment is not a thing of the past, but it is what takes them into their future!

There are singles who have been hurt in their relationships, whether in or outside the church. Perhaps this pain could have been lessened if we leaned not on our own understanding, but rather placed our trust and commitment in God, first and foremost.

Singles, irrespective of their gender, should hold close to their bosoms the fact that if there are commitment issues before marriage, a wedding, marriage certificate or a child will not fix those issues; in fact, they will likely exacerbate them. Total commitment starts with our trust and obedience to God. If we cannot commit and trust God, it will be hard, if not impossible, to trust anyone at all!

CHAPTER 3

DIVORCE: A BLESSING OR A SIN

Is Divorce under Law or Grace?

> *When a man hath taketh a wife and married her, and it came to pass that she find no favor in his eyes because he hath found some uncleanliness in her; Then let him write her bill of divorcement, and give it in her hand, and send her out of his house* (Deuteronomy 24:1).

Being a woman in biblical days was not a great experience. In those times, most women were seen as property and had few privileges. Hence, most of the laws were established to protect women from men treating them cruelly. The laws that women were subjected to back then are not adhered to by modern-day women.

Divorce was never the original plan of God. His desire is for husbands and wives to remain in the union until death do them part. However, after Adam sinned, mankind moved away from this principle for several reasons. In light of this, we see in the Old Testament, the institution of certain laws to discourage injustice against women who were vulnerable:

> *And when she is departed out of his house, she may go and be another man's wife. [3] And if the latter husband hate her, and write her a bill of divorcement, and giveth it in her hand, and sendeth her out of his house; or if the latter husband die, which took her to be his wife; [4] Her former husband, which sent her away, may not take her again to be his wife, after that she is defiled; for that is abomination before the Lord: and thou shalt not cause the land to sin, which the Lord thy God giveth thee for an inheritance.* (Deuteronomy 24:2-4).

Men in that day had unlimited freedom to divorce and remarry. All they had to do was make a public declaration. That gave the man freedom to divorce and remarry as many times as he saw fit. However, the woman had no such freedom. You can imagine the dire situation many women found themselves in.

In the preceding passage, we see the establishment of the law to protect women that if a man divorced a woman and she remarried, then the first man could never remarry her. The text also states that the man must have some sound reason to divorce. He needed to establish a reason, what is called "some indecency" (Dave Miller Jan, 27, 2012). In this context, the Hebrew word for "indecency" usually means "to expose the genitals," which is translated "nakedness." In Genesis 9:22, Ham, the son of Noah, "saw" the nakedness of his father.

Many years later, Jesus spoke about divorce in His teachings (See Matthew 19:3-12). However, we cannot add Jesus' teachings to Deuteronomy 24:2-4. The law had penalties for adultery, but divorce was not one of them. The penalty for either premarital or extramarital immorality was death (See Deuteronomy 22:20-22).

In his writing, "Divorce and Remarriage in the O.T.," Dave Miller (2012), looks at Jesus' response to the Pharisees concerning divorce. At that time, the Pharisaical groups, Shammai and Hillel, were at odds about the reasons a man had for divorcing his wife. The school of Shammai believed and taught that the "something indecent" was adultery or sexual immorality. Hence, a man could only divorce his wife if she was unfaithful to him. On the other hand, the school of Hillel took a more liberal approach. They taught that the man had the right to divorce his wife for any reason he chose e.g. her inability to cook as he desired, etc.

Consequent to the Pharisees' inquiry, Jesus spells out the grounds for divorce more clearly in the New Testament. Dave Miller lays out two deductions from Jesus' teachings:

1. Divorce may be sought for serious moral reasons
2. There are grounds upon which a divorce is biblically acceptable; divorce may not have been a part of God's original plan, but in a sinful world He makes allowances

We are living in a time where sin is a part of human life. Hence, people are fallible and make mistakes. Many people have gotten married for various reasons – right and wrong. As a result of certain decisions, many marriages end in divorce. It was God's original plan that the "two shall become one" and as stated earlier, they stay together until death do them part. However, it is noteworthy to highlight that sin had not entered man and the world when this covenant was established. The entrance of sin totally transformed mankind's nature, hence, creating issues that did not exist at the time of God's instructions. However, this does not in any way do away with the promise or lessen the commitment that one makes before God.

By no means is sin an escape from marriage. This is why one should not enter it lightly. Scripture makes us aware that where sin abides, grace abides more.

The Church: A Spiritual Hospital

> *And when the Pharisees saw it, they said unto his disciples, Why eateth your Master with publicans and sinner? But when Jesus heard that, he said unto them. They that be whole need not a physician, but they that are sick. But go ye and learn what they meaneth, I will have mercy and not sacrifice; for I am not come to call the*

righteous, but sinners to repentance (Matthew 9:11-13).

The body of Christ is a spiritual hospital for those who have asked for forgiveness. What is the primary reason for admittance into this hospital? It is being a sinner in need of Christ.

I have noticed from the time I was a child until now that the structures of most hospitals have not changed. Each floor or wing has a specific group of people who are treated there for a variety of reasons: cancer, childbirth, etc. Note, the patients are all under the same roof but on different floors depending on their specific problems.

You would often find on visiting the cancer floor or wing that most people there can relate to each other. They share stories of their experiences. They understand each other's concerns. However, when someone from the outside or another floor looks at that situation, it may seem as if those people should just move on. You see, the door leads in and out, and each floor is different.

> *But now the righteousness of God without the law is manifested, being witnessed by the law and the prophets; Even the righteousness of God which is by faith of Jesus Christ unto all and upon all them that believe; for there is no difference; For all have sinned and come short of the glory of God* (Romans 3:21-23).

As we keep with the analogy of the spiritual hospital, each floor has doctors who serve their patients. Many may say that those doctors don't have to be stricken with that particular ailment to serve. And I would not argue that point. However, each doctor must be trained to administer the right medicine and conduct themselves in an appropriate manner.

As spiritual doctors, we too should ensure that we are trained to administer the Word of God correctly. Many times, those of us called to be under-shepherds give the wrong scripture or word to the patients who are in dire need of something else. Consequently, we put people at risk. Suggesting to someone who lost his/her spouse or who was hurt in a relationship to just push through is inappropriate. It is a good word administered to the wrong patient.

The wrong word can cut the wrong artery. Administering the word must be done with precision so the patient does not bleed out and experience long-term pain that may lead to a hardened heart. For this reason, many people have left the church.

> *They say unto Him, Why did Moses then command to give a writing of divorcement and to put her away? He said unto them, Moses because of the hardness of your hearts suffered you to put away your wives: but from the beginning it was not so* (Matthew 19:7-8).

> The heart is the seal of emotion, intelligence, morality, human choice and one's religious life. The heart represents the total response of a person to life around him or her and to the religious and moral demands of God. Hardness of the heart thus describes a negative condition in which the person ignores, spurns or rejects the gracious office of God to be part of his or her life (*Baker Evangelical Dictionary of Biblical Theology*).

We all enter through the same door when we come to Christ. *"I am the door: by me if any man enters in, he shall be saved, and shall go in and out, and find pasture" (John 10:9).* There is no special door based on one's education, economic or marital status. Christ is the only way. He is the door that carries you in and out.

In the body of Christ (the spiritual hospital), the floor for those who have been hurt by divorce, death of a loved one, and being single has not been treated with care. Unfortunately, most of the time, these people are placed on floors with those who do not understand their specific needs.

When I first embarked on writing this book, being single through divorce was my purpose for writing. Since then, not only did my marriage fall apart, but the loss of my mother left me feeling single in my heart in another way. You can never understand how death and divorce can impact your life until you end up on that floor!

"Wherefore (as the Holy Ghost saith, today if ye will hear his voice, Harden not you hearts, as in the provocation, in the day of temptation in the wilderness" (Hebrews 3:7-8). If you have fallen into the despair of divorce or you have been widowed, you must first understand your situation is not a one-way ticket to a life of loneliness or punishment from God. And you are not without love and forgiveness. The Word of God and His love are here to release you from the sin and guilt. God will push you into a life of no regrets.

Feeling Lost After Divorce

"For the son of man has come to seek and to save that which was lost" (Luke 19:10). The Bible teaches that Jesus came for those who were lost in sin. Therefore, those of us who have been through the process of divorce have every right to be added to the body of Christ without being viewed as having committed the unforgivable sin.

In Luke 15, Jesus shares three parables about those who are lost: The Lost Sheep, The Lost Coin or Silver, and the Lost Son.

However, the church has paid special attention to recovering only two out of three.

The coin was lost in the house. In our churches, we have no problem reaching out to those in the house or to the son who spent all he had in the wrong place and returned home. But we ignore the sheep that was lost. For many reasons, the sheep wanted to eat by itself. Perhaps it felt left out, alone or it did not fit in and wandered off by itself. The plight of this sheep is the very one many believers face in the church. The single, divorced, and widowed are being left out; they are wandering off by themselves.

Those sheep have wandered away because of the indifference of the church and its stand on divorce. The law was given without the covenant of grace. The primary duty of the church is to embrace people, not on the law of God but the grace of God. Jesus answered the question that was presented to Him by those who upheld the law – the Pharisees.

> *They say unto him, Master, this woman was taken into adultery, in the very act. Now Moses in the law commanded us, that such should be stoned; but what sayest thou? This they said, tempting him that they might have to accuse him. But Jesus stooped down and with his finger wrote on the ground, as though he heard them not. So when they continued asking him, he lifted up himself, and said unto them, He that is without sin among you, let him first cast a stone at her* (John: 8:4-7).

> *But now the righteousness of God without the law is manifested, being witnessed by the law and the prophets; Even the righteousness of God which is by faith of Jesus Christ unto all and upon all them that believe: for there is no difference. For all*

> *have sinned, and come short of the glory of God*
> (Romans 3:21-23).

Jesus demonstrated that the grace of God overrides the law. For example, when the woman who was caught in adultery was brought to Him by the scribes and Pharisees, the law was addressed but the new covenant of grace was imputed.

Divorce should not be a mandate for the church to judge or to separate people from the body of Christ. It is true that each denomination has the right to govern the way it seems fit; however, please, do not 'invite people to the party' if you do not want them to receive all of the benefits.

> *What man of you, having an hundred sheep, if he lose one of them, doth not leave the ninety and nine in the wilderness, and go after that which is lost, until he find it? And when he hath found it, he layeth on his shoulders, rejoicing* (Luke 15:4-5).

It's time for the church, instead of ostracizing and sidelining those who are single, to go after them just as the shepherd sought the lost sheep. The greenery of life has made them wander away. Christ demonstrated the importance of that sheep. He showed the significance of pursuing those who feel lost and bringing them back into the fold.

Overcoming the Stigma of Divorce

After a divorce, we can find ourselves feeling depressed and lonely for many reasons. We may experience a rollercoaster of emotions that can make us feel like failures. However, because of the frequency of divorce in our culture, people tend to overlook the consequences of divorce and the signs that people, who have been divorced or have lost a spouse for some other reason, may be emotionally disturbed.

Many times, we do not take the time to heal and feel if we can just get into another relationship it will help us overcome the loneliness or depression we may be feeling. We think maybe having someone to go to dinner or a movie with can help us move past the hurt or loss that we are experiencing. These are real emotions that those who find themselves being single after many years in relationships may go through.

As I write this book, we heard the news that former president, George Bush's wife, of seventy plus years, passed away. The Sunday after the funeral, he was admitted to the local hospital near death. Those in the medical field said it was a "broken heart." This is a medical condition that we can experience after losing someone we love. No matter how toxic the relationship was your heart can be broken. Sometimes those around you will become frustrated by your grief whether through divorce or death and may feel you should just get over it. However, it's not that easy.

Divorce creates many questions. One nagging question that many ask is, "What happened?" They say, "I thought nothing could break you up." Those who are experiencing divorce think about these things every day and many times, answers to the questions cannot be found. Consequently, this leads to guilt.

I have always loved words and their meanings. So, let me take the liberty of presenting a definition of "guilt."

> Guilt is a cognitive or an emotional experience that occurs when a person believes or realizes – accurately or not – that he or she has compromised his or her own standards of conduct or has rotated a universal moral standard and bears significant responsibility for violation. Guilt is closely related to the concept of remorse (Wikipedia).

Over my years of counseling in the church, I have realized that sometimes, women who find themselves in abusive relationships feel guilty. Hence, they blame themselves for the behavior of the abuser. As a result, many women refuse to leave abusive relationships because they feel they can fix the problem.

In instances when they do find the courage to leave, many of these women carry lots of baggage with them. They are often scarred, not only physically but emotionally, mentally, and spiritually.

No one enters a relationship expecting it to fail or end in divorce. As they stand before God and those in authority to take those sacred vows, they do so with the intention that their marriages will last "until death do us part." However, as we know, not all marriages last, whether we feel God put us together or not. The question is not ours to ask. But everyone needs a second or even a third chance. *"Then came Peter to him and said, Lord how oft shall my brother sin against me, and I forgive him? Til seven times? Jesus saith unto him. I say not unto thee, Until seven times: but, Until seventy times seven"* (Matthew 18:21-22).

Members of the body of Christ should not be the ones who stigmatize those who have been through this painful act of divorce. Instead, we should seek to empathize and embrace the hurting.

Sad to say, with all the titles that are given out in today's churches, the one title we overlook is that of a "child of God." Christ still died for that one lost sheep that went astray.

No matter how those, who go through divorce, come out, whether on top or bottom, no one is a winner. The emotional damage is still there and if they enter a new relationship too soon, this will only add to the damage.

Only the Word of God can break through this pain or even the walls that have been built up. We must understand that on the surface, divorcees are now single, but beneath, they are still committed to those emotions. We must go through God's healing process to be made whole again. The apostle Paul gives us the Word of God for us to help:

> *Brethren, if a man be overtaken in a fault, ye which are spiritual, restore such a one in the spirit of meekness; considering thyself, lest thou also be tempted. Bear ye one another's burdens, and so fulfill the law of Christ* (Galatians 6:1-2).

We know under the old law, this sin of divorce was never to take place. We also know that the punishment for adultery and fornication was death. However, the law of Christ, though not advocating divorce, provides forgiveness. Christ died that *all* can be forgiven. Those who are divorced are no longer under the sin of the law, but the grace of God.

CHAPTER 4

LOOKING FOR LOVE IN ALL THE WRONG PLACES

A Need Driven Relationship

> *Not that I speak in respect of want; for I have learned, in whatsoever state I am, therewith to be content. I know both how to be abased, and I know how to abound; everywhere an in all things I am instructed both to be full and to be hungry, both to abound and to suffer need. I can do all things through Christ which strengthens me* (Philippians 4:11-13).

It is unrealistic to believe that those who belong to the body of Christ are only going to be attracted to others who are in the church.

Singles are faced with the decision of whether to commit to a relationship based on need. Paul addressed this in his letter to the Philippians. He said his thankfulness for their giving was not because he was in need but because it was good for them to be givers (even though Paul did need).

Many single women and men find themselves needy and sometimes fall into misguided relationships based on the desire to fulfill that need. As a result, they have unrealistic expectations from those supplying the need at the time.

Over the years, as a pastor, I have seen many single women who established very healthy relationships with Christ, the church, and the pastor being led out of the fold. This happened because they were so thirsty for a relationship, that they were willing to forfeit their spiritual and emotional growth.

The reality is that singles face many challenges with their sexual desires. They desire to be out of the waiting mode and married so this aspect of their lives can be fulfilled. However, as a single, one must realize that the temptations facing those who are married are not different from those who are single (not speaking sexually). These are what Christ speaks of in His address to the crowd in Matthew 6:24-34. Christ tells the crowd not to be anxious or weary about the basic or everyday needs and not to take thought for tomorrow.

The church must realize and admit that the basic needs of single people can force them into unhealthy relationships. Thus, leading to new definitions of what were once understood by both the church and the world as godly relationships.

Most of the time, in a two-person home – married or not – there are two incomes. Two people share the expenses of that home and contribute to meeting the basic needs of that family. When a person's basic needs are met, it is much easier to be content. However, singles have to meet their basic needs alone. The church must realize that being single is not a wish to be permissive but a wish to serve God without having to meet the basic needs on your own. In Genesis 2:1-25, God gives order for provision. Those provisions were made for Adam before He was created (Genesis 2:4-7).

In verse 7, God created mankind and placed a single man in the midst of the food or provisions. Then He gave the single man instructions on how to live. Afterward, He gave him a helpmate called woman. The point is that God met Adam's basic needs before he even addressed his state of loneliness. Likewise, the basic needs of singles must still be met even before the state of loneliness.

The basic needs of singles and married couples are primarily the same except that those who are married are in committed relationships where they can depend on each other for provisions.

> *These are the generations of the heavens and the earth when they were created, in the day that the Lord God made the earth and the heavens. And*

every plant of the field before it was in the earth, and every herb of the field before it grew: for the Lord God had not caused it to rain upon the earth, and there was not man to till the ground. But there went up a mist from the earth, and watered the whole face of the ground. And the Lord God formed man of the dust of the ground, and breathed into his nostrils the breath of life; and man became a living soul (Genesis 2:4-7).

A man who loves God should do everything he can to provide for the woman God gives him. This can take that relationship from just being one of contentment to one of satisfaction. Being satisfied is when you get or achieve what you want. Being content is being happy even if you don't get or achieve what you want.

Many relationships begin with both singles being content. Certain needs are being met in the relationship. However, it is only when the relationship goes to the next level that it can become satisfying or not. Don't take this the wrong way. In our relationship with God, we can be content with all He gives us. But as we mature in Him, and we see all His goodness, we begin to want more. It's doesn't mean we are greedy, just not satisfied with where we are.

It is so important to know that any relationship is going to grow. Therefore, as time goes on, we will want more than what we first had, not only physically but in all areas of the relationship. Having a good foundation with God is essential for couples to grow together.

Finding a Place to Worship

"My house should be called the house of prayer, but ye have made it a den of thieves" (Matthew 21:13). It is difficult not to

wonder when visiting many of our churches today, if God's house has become a social club where people meet and connect. There are so many social events, we label as ministries, that have taken the place of worship and the Word.

In some cases, the church has even gone as far as following the example of many dating sites. They are using these sites' marketing tools to bring singles into the church. As it relates to singles, divorced, and widows, in some instances, the church has become a place to meet and date, instead of fellowship. Those in authority have become the matchmakers and feel in many cases God has shown them who will make a perfect match.

Sadly, going to church has become more about connecting than worship. What happens if the relationship doesn't work? Do you see the potential for divisions and confusion in the church when it is made a matchmaking arena? Both individuals could leave the church if the relationship fails. Sometimes, they become so disillusioned they even sever their relationship with God.

As a married pastor, I would try to meet the needs or what I felt were the needs of singles. My method was to set up a singles' ministry to help singles socialize. They would meet and interact with Christian singles in the church. Now, they have Christian dating sites they can meet on. We would have singles' dinners, bowling, games, etc. I did this hoping they would connect and not feel lonely or left out when we, as married people, got together.

To my surprise, I discovered that most of the time, those singles did not show up to events planned for them by married people. And when they did meet someone, it was kept quiet so that the people in the church would not get involved if it did not work out.

I remember growing up as a young man, the older men on the job would tell me, "You don't get your money and honey from the same place." Well, I did not understand at the time, but what they were trying to say is that it is hard to date and work at the same place. It can be done, but once feelings and emotions become involved it can send a workplace into total chaos. That's why some employers separate couples once they are married. *"Be ye therefore wise as serpents, and harmless as doves"* (Matthew 10:16b).

God's house is a place to worship and should be treated that way. The intent on Sunday morning or on Bible study nights is not to play matchmaker for those who are single. If they do meet someone in the service, that's fine. These are two grown single adults who have heard the Word of God and experienced enough to make decisions on their own. It's their choice; they will deal with the outcomes. It's not the decision of the church and those in leadership to make.

The church must be very careful that it does not take on the mission and purpose of the world. I know as a pastor it's hard not to get involved in the personal lives of those we love and care about. We want them to be happy, in love, and have wonderful families. However, our purpose is to preach and teach the Word of God, not to meddle in people's affairs in unhealthy ways. We must let God's Word bring the healing people need in their lives.

Often, after Jesus ministered to the needs of people spiritually and physically, He would send them away. He would say to them, "Go and sin no more." It was as if He was telling them to go and live now that their lives were changed. The spiritual cleansing had taken place and they could have new beginnings.

"Preach the word; be instant in season, out of season; reprove, rebuke, exhort with all long-suffering and doctrine" (2 Timothy 4:2). The Apostle Paul wrote to His young pastor, Timothy, to

just preach the Word, no matter the status, economic position or ethics of the people in the church. Some will get it and some will not. Please do not misunderstand me. There should be special times set aside to address those who are single: conferences, seminars, etc. However, Sunday morning, in a mixed crowd, should not be the time to rebuke singles' lifestyles. It also should not be a time to exalt married couples for being married.

At the time of this writing, I have been divorced for ten years and a bishop for nine of those years. I can say that God has been good to me, but it didn't come without some pain and trials in my life.

The place I attend for worship is a place of freedom to let go of that hurt and pain from the week. It is not a place to meet and greet or be forced into a relationship I am not seeking.

Always remember that those who find themselves single are no different in their need to worship than those who are married.

God Will Position You in the Right Place

> *So Ruth the Moabites said to Naomi, "Please let me go to the field, and glean heads of grain after him in whose sight I may favor." And she said to her, "Go, my daughter." Then she left, and went and gleaned in the field after the reapers. And she happened to come to the part of the field belonging to Boaz, who was of the family of Elimelech. Now behold, Boaz came from Bethlehem, and said to the reapers. "The LORD be with you!" And they answered him, "The LORD bless you!" Then Boaz said to his servant who was in charge of the reapers, "Who young woman is this?* (Ruth 2:2-5).

Ruth's intentions were pure. Consequently, she was seen in the field (church) by Boaz. *"Therefore said he unto them, the harvest truly is great, but the labourers are few: pray ye therefore the Lord of the harvest, that he would send forth labourers into his harvest"* (Luke 10:2).

The church of the living God was never intended to be a place for social gatherings or to meet and greet for marriage and dating. Those who find relationships in these places are to cherish them but also remember that God's house is a place to worship Him.

As pastors, sometimes – or many times – we feel if we can place a person in a relationship that all his/her problems will go away. However, the opposite often occurs. The person takes past problems into their future relationship making it toxic.

"Whoso findeth a wife findeth a good thing, and obtaineth favor of the Lord" (Proverbs 18:22). The preceding passage leads one to believe that a wife is a token of God's divine favor. However, bliss in a marriage is not automatic.

> *And Ruth the Moabitess said unto Naomi, Let me go to the field and glean ears of corn after him in whose I shall find grace and favor. And she said unto her, Go, my daughter (Ruth 2:2). Ruth's intentions were pure and consequently, she was seen in the field by Boaz. Then she fell on her face, and bowed herself to the ground, and said unto him, Why have I found grace (Favor) in thine eyes, that thou shouldest take knowledge of me, seeing I am a stranger (Ruth 2:10).*

When God has placed two people in a relationship and our intentions are pure with God, then the grace or favor of God is upon that union. As Ruth positioned herself in a place to worship, both individuals will position themselves in a place to worship. They will not be in two separated fields (churches). But we do not want to overlook the fact that neither Ruth nor Boaz went to the fields with the intention of finding a relationship.

Ruth said to Naomi, *"Let me now go into the field and glean ear of corn."* This was a very profound statement. Ruth went to work. She just wanted provisions for Naomi and herself. Being obedient to the service of God, she was in the right place at the right time. My grandmother and mother used to tell me that if you look hard enough, you will find what you looking for. However, they failed to tell me you have to make sure you know what you are looking for.

If you are simply looking to be in a relationship, you will find what you are looking for. But, if you want a godly relationship, you must allow God to position you in the right field. This could be church, work, social events, etc.

"The earth is the Lord's, and the fullness there of; the world and they that dwell therein" (Psalm 24:1). It is still God's intent that we live long and joyful lives. Somewhere out there in His field is your Ruth or Boaz.

The Hosea Effect

"The beginning of the word of the Lord by Hosea. And the Lord said to Hosea, Go, take thee a wife of whoredoms and children of whoredoms; for the land hath committed great whoredom, departing from the Lord" (Hosea 1:2). As you can see, the relationship between Hosea and his wife is a contrast to the relationship between Ruth and Boaz. Sometimes, we enter relationships that seem not to be from the Lord. Just looking from the outside in, this relationship between Hosea and Gomer was doomed from the beginning. Those who looked on were perhaps shocked that Hosea the prophet would even consider marrying a prostitute. But it was a relationship ordained by God Himself. For the Lord compared their relationship to that of what the

people were doing in the land. It also warns us that if we are not careful, people and things around us can affect healthy relationships. Moreover, singles must separate themselves from toxic situations and outside relationships.

"What therefore God hath joined together, let no man put asunder" (Mark 10:9). In this verse, Jesus points out that marriage is not of human origin; it originated with God. And as mentioned earlier, divorce is not part of God's original plan for man. But Moses made allowance due to "hardness of heart" (Matthew 19:8).

If Hosea was in this toxic relationship today, many would say it's time to leave. Can you imagine the talk all around? How can this godly man keep putting up with this ungodly behavior? We must take note here that Hosea and Gomer were not physically abusive to each other. Under no circumstances should anyone stay in that kind of relationship.

In the Hosea Effect, we can see perceived incompatibilities in someone else's relationship and say it's not of God. We conclude that God would never put the two people together. Furthermore, we may say that if we were in that relationship, we would leave.

Hosea had the grace of God over his life to endure in his marriage to Gomer. He knew his love for Gomer surpassed anything that she had done, and he was willing to place his life on the line to fulfill his vow to her.

As singles enter relationships, there will always be issues that each person brings into the relationship. Gomer could not let go of her past and was always trying to recapture what seemed to escape her. Hosea was self-righteous and never felt he had done anything to deserve what was happening to him. But both had to submit to the love and will of God to make that relationship work.

"Husbands, love your wives, even as Christ also loved the church, and gave himself for it" (Ephesians 5:25). With the Hosea Effect, a man who finds a wife can give himself to her as Christ did for the church. Admittedly, this doesn't start after the vows, but must be there throughout the relationship.

> *And the Lord God caused a deep sleep to fall upon Adam, and he slept; and he took one of his ribs, and closed up the flesh instead thereof; And the rib, which the Lord God had taken from man, made he a woman, and brought her unto the man. And Adam said, "This is now bone of my bones, and flesh of my flesh; she shall be called woman because she was taken out of man." Therefore shall a man leave his father and his mother, and shall cleave unto his wife: and they shall be one flesh* (Genesis 2:21-24).

This is a picture of marital intimacy. It's when you transition from being single to being married. To *"cleave"* means to adhere to, stick to, or join with. Leaving one's parents means recognizing that your marriage created a new family and this family takes priority over your previous family.

Many singles are asking God for spouses, and I believe God will honor their requests. Nonetheless, like Hosea, are both parties ready to take that next step? Are they willing to leave and cleave?

Many Christian parents are uncomfortable releasing their Christian children into their new relationships. They are afraid to let go. However, if they don't, it can be very damaging to the new couple. Parents must give their children room to build new families as God has ordained. Remember, they were once single, now, they are married. Like Hosea and Gomer, there must be a time for God to intervene and work out their relationship.

This story is one of unfailing love; no matter what his wife's past was, Hosea loved her. It is also a story of God's unfailing love for His people and the world.

Singles must ask themselves these questions about the love they have for each other before they say, "I do."

1. Do I love this person unconditionally?
2. Can I can forget his/her past and the struggles we may have?
3. Is it the love that the Apostle Paul speaks of?

"And now abideth faith, hope, charity, (love) these three; but the greatest of these is charity, (love) (1 Corinthians 13:13).

CHAPTER 5

THE PITFALLS OF SINGLE LIFE

The Pitfalls of Single Life

> *And it came to pass, when Joseph was come unto his brethren, that they strip Joseph out of his coat, his coat of many colors that was on him. And they took him, and cast him into a pit: and the pit was empty, there was no water in it* (Genesis 37:23-24).

The story is told in Genesis 37 of a young man named Joseph who had dreams of being great. However, his brothers tried to prevent him from reaching those goals because of jealousy. Eventually, he was thrown into a pit and sold into slavery. His journey was not what he chose. Most likely, he would have preferred a different course.

Many people are not single by choice. They did not choose this lifestyle on their own. If it was all up to them, they would not be single. However, as we know, life happens. Dreams and hopes are drowned by the circumstances of life. Many people are single because they were thrown into the pit of divorce, widowed or separated because of unforeseen circumstances.

These pitfalls can cause low self-esteem and even depression. Therefore, as they enter places of worship, they must be built up, not pulled down. They need to feel accepted and a part of the worship experience. Too often in our churches, pastors and other married people focus more on sin in the lives of single people than on the pit they are in. They don't take the time to reach out to these individuals, to understand the pain they are feeling and to show their concern.

If a person is in a pit – including someone who is single – the first priority is to get him/her out, not criticize and condemn the person. Extend a hand of love.

If you are a single parent, you must try by any means necessary to bring your family out of the pit, as well.

Feelings of loneliness and depression can lead people to consider getting into ungodly and unprofitable relationships. There is a pressing need for companionship, which they want satisfied at any cost.

Single people may also feel their spiritual and social lives are getting fed, but their commitment to a solid relationship is not there. They settle for the two out of three, not knowing that relationship will affect all areas of their lives. They hope and dream that one day the person with whom they are in a relationship will finally make a commitment to them even if it means being unequally yoked. Hence, the cycle of trying to come out begins. Each time they make an effort, their hopes of having a perfect person in their lives is diminished.

Certainly, the church has to admit its role in propagating the illusion of perfection. It has painted a picture of Christians having perfect marriages. Pastors have taught that at some time in the future, God will send the perfect person with all the God-given attributes that are mentioned in the scriptures for the single Christian. Furthermore, the marriage of such a person will be eternally blissful.

Unfortunately, many pastors and other married people in the church have failed to be transparent and truthful about their marital and other experiences. They don't open up enough to let others see the reality of life – no couple is perfect and marriage is a day by day, week by week and year by year relationship that must be worked on. Singles should be counseled that the best preparation for their marriage is to establish a committed relationship with Christ. In doing so, you can avoid the pitfalls of the relationship. In the event that pitfalls present themselves and you fall down, God can bring you out.

Unlike what many believe, this does not come by holding special programs for adult singles. Most adult singles have lives outside of the walls of the church. In fact, many singles only come to church to get involved in ministry and worship.

Below are some of the pitfalls you may find yourself in as a single person. You will note they are not much different from the pitfalls of those who are married.

Low Self-esteem

Singles with low self-esteem often lack confidence in themselves because of the stigma that comes with not being in a committed relationship . They tend to feel unlovable and badly about who they are and think they will never get married. As a result, the person may be uncertain that God has the best for him/her, not only in a relationship but in all areas of life.

Settling for Anyone and Anything

Settling for anyone and anything not to feel lonely or to fit in is a number one pitfall for singles. It can be a challenge staying focused and contented with singleness when everyone around is either married or in a committed relationship. Therefore, many singles resign to the belief that getting involved with anyone is better than having no one. They may also believe that companionship of some sort would get rid of their feelings of inadequacy. Unfortunately, if the relationship does not work, many people remain in the union because they feel they cannot do better. They choose to stay in the pit.

The Sense of Feeling Lonely or Alone

"And the LORD God said, It is not good that the man should be alone; I will make him an help meet for him" (Genesis 2:18). It is important to understand that Scripture must be kept in the context in which it was written first before being applied to our lives. Remember that God had provided for Adam's basic needs before He gave him a wife as a helpmeet. Moreover, sin had not entered the earth. God showed Adam that he could not do it by himself; he had a need. Therefore, God brought Adam into a relationship with the woman.

In the world today, the need for a relationship is still there but because of sin, how we connect in these relationships can be hurtful. Adam's first relationship was with God and then the woman. We should follow this example and seek fulfillment in God before we pursue romantic relationships with others. That desire to feel loved must be handled with discipline. That's why the church must teach – not only to the singles – but to all that you can feel alone even when you are married.

Not Taking Time to Get to Know Each Other

Rushing into a relationship is a major pitfall that has created many problems in people's lives. Sometimes we are so eager to date and fit in with the others who are doing so that we accept the first person who shows interest – good or bad. However, Scripture tells us to be careful for nothing (anxious); but in everything by prayer and supplication with thanksgiving let your requests be known unto God (See Philippians 4:6).

Dating has taken on new meanings in the world we live in today. And these meanings are being played out in single lives in the church. I have spoken to many pastors, families, and Christian friends asking them how long they've been married (from 10-30 more years). In doing so, I have discovered that many of them met in various ways: on the job, school, and some even shared God brought them together even before they met. They say God told them who their wives or husbands would be. So, they speak to singles from their own experiences about what may have worked or not.

All marriages have one thing in common – problems. That's a fact. Don't be fooled by appearances. In fact, things are seldom the way they appear to be. Any honest, married couple will tell you that problems do occur. Many have expressed they wished they had known more about their spouses before marriage. Not that they don't love the person but getting to know the person you're spending the rest of your life with is important – bone of my bone.

Moving through the Hurt of the Past

> *Let no man say when he is tempted, I am tempted of God; for God cannot be tempted with evil, neither tempteth he any man. But every man is tempted, when h is drawn away of his own lust, and enticed. Then when lust have conceived, it bringeth forth sin; and sin, when it is finished, bring forth death* (James 1:13-15).

In my years of pastoring, I have experienced many people who did not take time to heal from past relationships. Many times when this occurs, they play the blame game. They see and rehearse all the other person's faults but never examine what drew them into the relationship in the first place. Was it God or being tempted outside of the will of God? The idea that one can have a perfect relation without being tempted by some outside factor is unrealistic.

The Rahab Pitfall

"And they went, can came into an harlot's house, named Rahab, and lodged there" (Joshua 2:1). The Bible tells us about Rahab, a prostitute, who took two spies and hid them from the king of Jericho. Of course, no one would have expected God to use a prostitute to fulfill His purpose, but He did. We are very good at labeling and stereotyping people based on our perceptions. However, we must understand that labeling anyone is wrong.

Singles face the problem of labeling in the church time and time again. Some of them shy away from getting involved in ministry because of how those in the church may view them based on their past. In fact, what I have noticed from my experience is that singles do not pair up with those who are married because they don't want others to think they are trying to tempt another person's spouse. Instead of going through the hassle of dealing with the attitudes of people's spouses, they prefer not to get involved.

Single women also do not want to feel they are leading men on or be accused of being involved in ministry for ulterior motives. Hence, they simply attend service and leave after it's over. Because of that approach, no relationships are built through fellowship, and it is easy to stay in the trap of no commitment in other areas of life. If you want to see what a true relationship looks like, you must be seriously dedicated to God and the house of God.

Repeating the Old Cycle

> *"Brethren, I count not myself to have apprehended: but this one thing I do, forgetting those things which are behind, and reaching forth unto those things which are before"* (Philippians 3:13).

We have all experienced relationships that have left us hurt. The wounds were very painful. In my personal experience, I would classify some hurt as good and some bad. However, I also admit that both have left me stronger when dealt with in positive ways.

The Scripture reminds us that no matter what our situation, God is always with us. He is ever present in whatever place or state of mind we find ourselves. We cannot succumb to repetitive behaviors that lead us into toxic relationships. Leaving some memories behind is the best choice we can make. It can help strengthen the next relationship we enter. People are different, so everyone we meet will have varying strengths and weaknesses, likes and dislikes, good and bad ways. The reality is we can control no one but ourselves. Therefore, we need to search ourselves and see where we need to make changes so we do not carry old problems into new relationships.

I dedicated this last chapter to avoiding pitfalls, but I am also aware that just like Joseph, God will allow us to fall into some pitfalls of life.

Understandably, some pitfalls are to reposition us to the next level of grace that God has for us. After Joseph had finished with the 37th chapter of his life and went through some rough times, even being accused of raping another man's wife and being thrown into prison, life started to change. Before he got to the 45th chapter of his life where he revealed who he was to his family, God had restored him. The point is that we must go through different chapters in life.

God allowed Joseph to reach his purpose and to fulfill his dream. As he looked back over his past, he connected it with his future and then he revealed who he was. All the hurts and pain of the pitfalls were now his strength. He could enter a new relationship with the old and new.

As Joseph showed through his actions, my prayer is that as singles, we can show through our actions that we are living life with no regrets.

I want to close with the Word of God from the Preacher in the Song of Solomon: *"I returned and saw under the sun, that the race is not to the swift, nor the battle to the strong, neither yet bread to the wise, nor yet riches to men of understanding, nor yet favor to men of skill; but time and chance happened to them all"* (Ecclesiastes 9:11).

"And the second liken unto the first: But he that shall endure unto the end, the same shall be saved" (Matthew 24:13). I remember joining a church as a young man in Durham North Carolina and being in the young adult choir. We sang a song that stated, *"This World Is Not My Home; I Am Just Passing Through."* At that time, those words did not have much meaning to me. Life was full of young hope, dreams, and relationships. The thought of failing at any of these was not an option. Now, as the years have passed and not all my dreams have come true, I understand what the elder people meant when they said, "Take life one day at a time and enjoy every minute of it."

Life presents many opportunities to enter and build relationships. How and what we bring to those relationships can help or hurt us. Over the years, I have learned that every relationship must start at one point and end at another even if that end is when someone we love passes into the arms of God.

Writing this book has helped me look backward and forward in relationships. I have had occasions to examine myself to see the areas that needed improvement. I have learned looking back and going back are two different things. You can't live in the past. You can only live in the present and look forward to what the future holds.

Living single and saved is not a curse on your life. It is not a sign that something is wrong with you. Rather, it is a place in God that you must embrace and live like you never lived before. Enjoy life because this world is not your home. We are just passing through.

The race is not given to the swift, those who get married or find that special someone before you – not even those who obtain the riches of this life. But this race is for those who, when they reach that finish line of life, can look back and say, "I live the single and saved life with no regrets."

POSTLUDE

Living alone can be tough on anyone. Getting the essentials in life, on its own, will leave one stressed and frustrated. Those who find themselves in this situation sometimes turn to any means they can to overcome life's obstacles. As such, trying to make it on your own without the support of family or the church is problematic.

While living single and saved, having a relationship with God can and should be a source of comfort, because I know one thing for certain: the daily struggles of life are common to the saved and unsaved alike!

A single can be judged differently on how she/he handles these struggles when, for example, she/he tries to find love in the wrong place; after all, whether outside the church or in the confinement of the House of God, *"He that loveth not knoweth not God; for God is love"* (1 John 4:8). Words cannot describe how awesome it is to know that God love all of us equally, no matter what our status in life.

There are many reasons that you may find yourselves being single. Some of those reasons may be by our hand. Others may be beyond our control or reach. Either way, as singles, we must learn to embrace the moment, and be secure in that knowledge that this too will pass, and that our lives can change dramatically in an instant. Loving oneself is the key to the love of God in one's life.

Over the years, churches have not embraced singles and have actually shunned them for various reasons. Many churches are of the view that singles cannot be in leadership roles because not having a spouse is, somehow, indicative of a lack of discipline. Some churches consider singles to be uncontrollable in their lives and are fearful that they would bring that unhinged spirit with them into the church.

These feelings hurt the church's growth, and that of the singles who are yearning to grow spiritually.

I must say, though, that not all churches have this disdain for singles. Several have found positive ways to include singles into their ministry. Some have reached out to the singles, not with the view to understanding singlehood, but rather to get idea of what they have to face by themselves.

> *And thou shall love the Lord thy God with all Thy heart, and with all thy soul, and with all thy mind, and with all thy strength; this is the first commandment. And the second is like, namely this, thou shalt love thy neighbor as thyself. There is none other commandment greater than these* (Mark 12:30-31).

Being single can have you looking more to your outside situation than dealing with the emotions than can accompany the status of being the sole provider in your home. Our circumstances can often dictate our emotions and leave us hopeless. The first step is to love oneself, God, and each other, to conquer that feeling of loneliness.

Satan wants to make you feel unloved and unwanted as singles and more so as a person. A person who has unreliable friends will eventually find herself/himself without those friends, especially at a time when she/he needs them the most… but there is a friend who sticks closer than a brother, no matter what the trial or tribulation. His name is Jesus.

No matter how you become single, the resulting struggles are real.

In this book, as a single you will discover how to deal with those struggles so that you can enjoy your life until God places you in the right situation. As you read it, you will understand that God loves everyone and never judges us on our past relationships. You will see that being in a relationship, just because, can be toxic, and that loving oneself first and foremost is the key to any prosperous relationship. You will learn about all the pleasures of life, and how not to live it to please others. You will come to understand that real joy originates from the inside and spreads outwards; not the outside going in.

Why wait for your soul mate when God has a wealth of things for your soul to enjoy in the meantime? In Christ all things are new; the things that made you happy in the past may not bring you any joy now, in the new you!

Losing a loved one, or going through a divorce, can lead to a myriad of emotions... but as you turn the pages of your life, my prayer is that you can take comfort knowing the Word of God speaks to those who feel alone and are separated from their loved ones. This means that we can always be confident knowing that while we are at home in the body, we are absent from the Lord (for we walk by faith, not by sight). We are confident, I say, and willing rather to be absent from the body, and to be present with the Lord (See 2 Cor. 5:6-8).

Having a loved one pass away may be difficult to come to terms with, but we are given the assurance that they are with the Lord and our faith in God must surpass the feelings of abandonment we are experiencing.

As a single person, God's assurance is what we must have confidence in until we meet that special person that God sends our way once again; not to fill a void, but to take us to the next level of His Glory.

It takes an astounding level of maturity to not become unhinged by every person we meet and who is prophesied to us in consideration of a new relationship. Let's keep looking to the hills which cometh out help, knowing that all our help come from the Lord.

Brethren, I count not myself to have apprehend: but this one thing I do, forgetting those things which are behind, and reaching forth unto those things which are before.

"I press toward the mark for the prize of the high calling of God in Christ Jesus" (Phil. 3:13-14). There can be no doubt that letting go of the past and pressing forward when you are single and saved can almost feel like an impossibility. My prayer and hope are that as you read this book, the Holy Spirit will guide you through those difficult times when you cannot help but look back at what used to be.

The purpose of this book is not to help you find a mate but to keep you until God brings that special person into your life. This book will teach you how, when you look back, not to do so with any regrets.

ABOUT THE AUTHOR

Bishop Daryl B. Anderson was born in Durham, North Carolina. He received his call to ministry and was ordained in Austin, Texas in 1986. He served as Associate and Youth Pastor for several ministries until 1990. In January of 1991, he founded New Life Christian Center in his apartment building with a few of his loyal family members. He obtained a Bachelor's Degree in Biblical Studies from Beulah Heights University, a Certificate of Business from Clark Atlanta University, Master's degree from Luther Rice Seminary, and an Honorary Doctorate of Divinity Degree from St. Thomas Christian University. During his advanced education endeavors, he was inducted into the Beta Kappa Society, designated Cum Laude, and received the Cambridge Award of Who's Who.

Bishop Anderson was consecrated Bishop in 2007 by the late Archbishop Jimmie Lee Smith, and served as the Bishop of Finance for the Light of the World Interdenominational International Association. He has presided over Georgia, North Carolina, Liberia, West Africa and Swaziland, Southeast Africa. He has also brought the Word of God to Mexico, the Caribbean, London, and Rome and has since established several ministries in the Rome, Georgia area along with an internet ministry in Pakistan.

Bishop Anderson works as the Spiritual Advisor with the Atlanta Gospel Fest, and has traveled extensively in the past with legendary gospel vocalists, Dorothy Norwood and Shirley Caesar.

Bishop Anderson's vision is to bridge the gap between the church and the community. As the current Deputy Director of Chaplain Services with the Cobb County Prison System, he serves as a counselor for inmates. He has taken courses under the Georgia

Sheriff's Association and has received the Law Enforcement Chaplain's Certification. His community ministry addresses issues relating to at-risk teens, battered women, and drug addiction. He also has worked to established youth programs with former Governor of Georgia, Roy Barnes. On behalf of the City of Rome, Georgia Board of Commissioners, he was awarded a Proclamation in 2010.

In May of 2009, Bishop Anderson started Word of Life Ministries in Rome, Georgia and with its continued growth, he moved into a larger establishment to accommodate members in Rome and the surrounding areas. In 2016, he felt the call of God to become an ambassador for Shiloh Worship Centre in London England.

Bishop Anderson is a dedicated father and grandfather to his daughters and grandchild, respectively. He believes in putting God first in his life, and lives by Phil.4:13, *"I can do all things through Christ which strengthens me."*

For speaking engagements or book signings, please contact Bishop Anderson using the information below.

Bishop Daryl B. Anderson
770-891-1338
pastordanderson@yahoo.com
Facebook: Bishop Daryl Anderson
Instagram: Bishop Daryl Anderson

www.ingramcontent.com/pod-product-compliance
Lightning Source LLC
Chambersburg PA
CBHW052114070526
44584CB00017B/2484